Gabriel Caldas Barros e Sá
Náthalee Cavalcanti de Almeida Lima

LOOP ACADEMIC EDUCATIONAL*SOFTWARE*

Gabriel Caldas Barros e Sá
Náthalee Cavalcanti de Almeida Lima

LOOP ACADEMIC EDUCATIONAL*SOFTWARE*

STUDENT MODULE *FRONT-END* DEVELOPMENT

ScienciaScripts

Imprint

Any brand names and product names mentioned in this book are subject to trademark, brand or patent protection and are trademarks or registered trademarks of their respective holders. The use of brand names, product names, common names, trade names, product descriptions etc. even without a particular marking in this work is in no way to be construed to mean that such names may be regarded as unrestricted in respect of trademark and brand protection legislation and could thus be used by anyone.

Cover image: www.ingimage.com

This book is a translation from the original published under ISBN 978-620-2-80764-7.

Publisher:
Sciencia Scripts
is a trademark of
International Book Market Service Ltd., member of OmniScriptum Publishing Group
17 Meldrum Street, Beau Bassin 71504, Mauritius

ISBN: 978-620-3-30017-8

Copyright © Gabriel Caldas Barros e Sá, Náthalee Cavalcanti de Almeida Lima
Copyright © 2021 International Book Market Service Ltd., member of OmniScriptum Publishing Group

I dedicate this work to my beloved and dear parents, especially my mother, who always gave me strength and supported me even from a distance, being the person who inspires me to move forward and never give up my dreams.

"Hard work wins the natural gift."

(Rock Lee)

Acknowledgements

Above all, I thank God for giving me strength to face the difficulties and to continue day after day in this hard battle that is life, for allowing me to be able to conquer things that I never imagined I would achieve. Thank you, Father, for always being by my side.

I am especially grateful to my dear teacher, Dr. Náthalee Cavalcanti, who was very important in my decision to continue in the area of Computer Engineering. For all the lessons, for the patience and great help in developing this work, which is something totally new to me. Thank you for being beyond a great teacher, a great person!

I can't forget to thank all the LABIE staff, students and teachers, who welcomed me and actively participated in the elaboration of this monograph, especially the teachers Dr. Laysa Mabel and Me. Jarbele Coutinho, as well as Professor Náthalee, who is also part of the group, who were always willing to help me when I needed it.

I leave my thanks to the student Dyego Magno for starting this beautiful project, which I am continuing, and for making himself available to assist me, as well as the other students from LABIE.

With great affection, I thank Professor Dr. Hidalyn Theodory, who has helped me countless times since I entered the university and who shows great affection for the profession. I feel honored to have been his student!

I also thank the friends I made when I joined UFERSA, who made this hard road become a little lighter with all the moments of fun and also study, especially to Thiago Aquino, José Lira (the late Ben 10), Felipe William, Fagner Rezende, Yam Souto and José Luan.

My wife and my father, who even with all the difficulties of life, was always willing to help me in the way he could.

Finally, I thank the most special person in my life: my mother, Cida, the reason for my existence, the strongest and most perfect woman I know, the woman who would give her life for me. Without her I wouldn't have gotten that far and I wouldn't be able to tread my dreams. She was the one who always encouraged me to study, to move forward, guided me in the tiring paths and supported me in my decisions. It was her who made me be the man I am today, and I hope to become at least 10% of the person she is. Thank you, mainha, I love you!

SUMMARY

A large proportion of computer and technology students face difficulties in the introductory programming disciplines, and this reflects the lack of preparation for the job market. To alleviate this problem, which also occurs in the most diverse areas of teaching, Educational *Software* has been used as a means to assist both the student and the teacher in the teaching-learning process. Therefore, this work seeks to develop the *Client Side* of the main functionalities of the Student module of the Educational Software *web* named *Loop Academic*, developed in HTML5, CSS, *JavaScript* and other tools, whose target are the students of the curricular components that involve introductory programming. For this purpose, the methodology used consists of the choice of *web* development tools, study of the already existing prototype of the Student module, selection of the main functionalities and, finally, the codification of the *front-end,* resulting in a static system that will serve as a basis for future complementary work aimed at developing the other components of the *Software*.

Keywords: Development, *web*. *Software,* Educational. Programming.

Front-End. Informatics in Education.

LIST OF ABBREVIATIONS AND ACRONYMS

AJAX	*Asynchronous JavaScript And XML*
API	*Application Programming Interface*
CAPES	Coordination of Improvement of Higher Level Personnel
CSS	*Cascading Style Sheets*
DOM	*Document Object Model*
HTML	*Hyper Text Markup Language*
IDE	*Integrated Development Environment*
JIT	*Just-in-Time*
LABIE	Laboratory of Research in Informatics in Education
MOJO	*Online* Judges Integration Mode
POO	Object Oriented Programming
PPV	Visual Programming Platform
REDU	Educational Social Network
SE	Educational *Software*
SO	Operating System
SVG	*Scalable Vector Graphics*
UFERSA	Federal Rural University of Semi-Arid
UFScar	Federal University of São Carlos
W3C	*World Wide Web Consortium*

SUMMARY

Acknowledgements 3
SUMMARY 5
LIST OF ABBREVIATIONS AND ACRONYMS 7
1.   INTRODUCTION 11
OBJECTIVES 12
GENERAL OBJECTIVE 12
SPECIFIC OBJECTIVES 12
ORGANIZATION OF WORK 13
2.   THEORETICAL REFERENCE 14
2.1. INFORMATION TECHNOLOGY IN EDUCATION 14
2.3. ACADEMIC LOOP 16
2.4. WEB DEVELOPMENT 16
   2.4.1.   FRONT-END 17
   2.4.1.2   CSS 19
      2.4.1.3   JAVASCRIPT 20
      2.4.1.4   BOOTSTRAP FRAMEWORK 22
      2.4.1.5   jQUERY 23
3.   RELATED WORKS 25
4.   METHODOLOGY 27
4.1. CHOICE OF TOOLS 27
4.2. STUDY OF THE STUDENT MODULE PROTOTYPE 31
4.3. SELECTION OF THE MAIN FUNCTIONALITIES 31
4.4. CODIFICATION 32
5.   RESULTS AND DISCUSSIONS 33
6.   FINAL CONSIDERATIONS 45
7.   REFERENCES 46
8.   ANNEX A - HTML Code 52

1. INTRODUCTION

A significant proportion of students enter the labor market still somewhat unprepared, and this is reflected in the growing dissatisfaction of the industry with this fact, which prompts educational institutions, especially universities, to reinvent themselves and seek new methods to make the teaching-learning process more effective (CALLAHAN; PEDIGO, 2002).

Especially in the teaching of computer programming in technology courses, such as *Software Engineering*, Computer Engineering, Computer Science, among others, the so-called Educational *Software* (SEs) have been used as a way to help the student's learning process. According to Jucá (2006), SEs are any programs inserted and used appropriately in education, both in teaching and learning. Oliveira et al. (2001) also classify the EHs in two ways: applications, which have no educational purpose but can be used for this purpose, as text editors; and the educational, which are developed specifically to help teaching-learning.

The use of SEs in Brazil was initially instigated by what was happening in countries like France and the United States of America, where the use of computer tools in the academic environment was already being applied. Then, in the 70s, the University of São Carlos (UFScar) pioneered the insertion of *software* in its teaching and study mechanisms (PENHA, 2015). In view of the rapidly evolving technological scenario, which demands more and more effectiveness and efficiency in learning, the use of ES in order to complement conventional teaching has proven to be a practical and useful way out. According to Jucá (2006), these technologies serve as a support in the teaching-learning process and university professors should be able to evaluate when they should use them and what benefits they can bring to the construction of knowledge.

Basic computer knowledge has become extremely necessary in today's society. Therefore, it is important that teaching be able to provide the specific skills so that the individual can have the perception and interaction with the technological evolution of everyday life (JUCÁ, 2006). In the introductory programming disciplines, this is even more relevant, considering that, according to Gomes (2010), there are a high number of cases of failure in them all over the world, regardless of the programming language used. This is also noticeable from the analysis of data obtained in research conducted by Holland (2018), where almost half of the students of the disciplines of Algorithms, Laboratory of Algorithms and Applied Informatics declared having difficulties in programming logic and understanding the syntax.

The main difficulty students face in programming subjects is logical reasoning, which also becomes a great challenge for teachers, who need to deal with classes of students with different levels of knowledge, in addition to the gap in basic content, such as mathematics, which is closely linked to logic (SOARES;

CARVALHO, 2017).

The teaching-learning of computer programming is one of the greatest difficulties faced within the technology courses (CASPERSEN and KOLLING, 2009). Because of this, the use of SE is beneficial and useful, because, according to the Market (2002), an SE is a didactic-pedagogical resource that serves as a support to the teacher in the mission of teaching and in the student's learning process. Lima et al. (2012) says that the number of national SE has grown due to constant technological innovations and the perception that the use of computers positively influences education. In addition, EHs can be developed for numerous platforms and operating systems according to focus and need, which makes them very flexible.

According to Carita, Sanches and Padovan (2011), the new paradigm of society, called the Information Society, is based on the use of technology as a mediator for obtaining and disseminating knowledge. Therefore, knowing how to take advantage of these technologies aimed at education is a real need of educational institutions today, as each generation becomes more connected (PENHA, 2015).

In view of the facts highlighted above, one can see the importance of the development of SEs aimed at the introductory programming of computers. In this way, when we realize the difficulty faced by many students in the introductory programming disciplines and the benefits that an SE can bring to both students and teachers, this work aims to minimize this problem situation by developing a means, in this case, the *front-end* of an *online* platform characterized as an educational type SE. The system should serve as an aid to both students and teachers of the curricular components that involve introductory computer programming by facilitating and dynamizing the teaching and learning of the same.

OBJECTIVES

In this section, the general objective and the specific objectives of this research are presented.

GENERAL OBJECTIVE

This work has the purpose of performing the *web* development in the *client side* axis, also called *front-end*, of the Student module present in the documentation and prototype of SE called *Loop Academic,* presented in the work done by student Dyego Magno Oliveira Souza[1] , whose target audience are students of disciplines focused on introductory computer programming.

SPECIFIC OBJECTIVES

In order to achieve the general objective, the specific objectives have been

---
[1] Souza, Dyego (2019)

defined and are listed below:

I. To promote the analysis of the importance of an SE and its influence on the teaching-learning process both in general and applied to the teaching of introductory programming;

II. Carry out a study of the main languages and tools for *web* development, some of them being HTML, CSS and *JavaScript*;

III. Define both languages (markup, *script* and alike) and the Integrated Development Environment (IDE) and external tools (such as *Frameworks* and *Libraries*) in order to use them to develop the

SE according to the existing prototype and also according to the specific objective II;

IV. Carry out a thorough analysis of the functionalities present in the Student module from the study of the documentation and its prototype, with the purpose of selecting the main ones so that they have their *front-end* developed.

ORGANIZATION OF WORK

This work is organized as follows: In chapter 2, the theoretical framework is arranged and divided into three parts of greatest relevance: section 2.1 analyzes information technology in education; section 2.2 explains the ESS in general and section 2.3 gives a brief explanation of *web* development, the latter still being divided into six subsections: section 2.2.3.1 focuses on the *front-end*, 2.3.1.1 presents HTML, while subsections 2.3.1.2 and 2.3.1.3 deal with CSS and *JavaScript,* respectively, while 2.3.1.4 explores the *Bootstrap framework* and 2.3.1.5, the *jQuery library*. Chapter 3 deals with the work related to this, while section 4 presents the methodology and is divided into four sections: section 4.1 justifies the choice of tools, section 4.2 presents the study of the prototype of the Student module, section 4.3 presents the main functionalities selected and section 4.4 deals with the process of coding the system. Chapter 5 presents the results and discussions obtained during this work where, in section 5.1, the results of the *front-end* development are displayed. Finally, chapter 6 provides the final considerations and proposals for future work.

2. THEORETICAL REFERENCE

This chapter provides a review and analysis of what the literature presents regarding the three main themes addressed in this research, being Informatics in Education, Educational *Software* and *Web* Development.

2.1. INFORMATION TECHNOLOGY IN EDUCATION

In general, education should consist of the student's search for information, its use for problem solving and the transformation of that information into knowledge, and not just another instruction that the teacher transmits to the student (VALENTE, 2014). Silva and Serafim (2016, p. 72) consider that "digital media have an enormous potential for teaching, but it is difficult to realize this potential if they are considered only technologies and not forms of culture and communication", and also that "[...] technologies do not replace the teacher, but can enable changes in their methodology".

It is important to stress that technology has always been important to society, especially as a way of spreading knowledge. Koile and Singer (2006) emphasize that the use of technology in education significantly improves student learning. Brito Junior (2016) emphasizes that "the combination of Education and Technology results in opportunities for growth in the teaching-learning process", and also that information and communication technologies are added to education in order to significantly improve the teaching-learning process.

In fact, the development of science and, consequently, technology, has generated changes in the interaction between the school and the student, presenting the need for the implementation of new media in education, where these tools should serve as learning facilitators (DIOGINIS et al., 2015), that is, the use of these tools, especially those focused on information technology, has become increasingly useful and necessary in the educational environment.

Nevertheless, the teacher's assistance in creating ideal learning environments for the student is essential, using, in addition to conventional methods, information technology alone does not generate knowledge, but the way these resources are used (KOCH, 2013). However, the teaching-learning process depends mostly on the student, because, according to Moran (2000, p-17-18):

> Changes in education also depend on students. Curious and motivated students greatly facilitate the process, stimulate the teacher's best qualities, become lucid interlocutors and walking partners of the teacher-educator. Motivated students learn and teach, advance further, help the teacher to help them better.

Regarding the teaching of introductory programming, which is the focus of SE development in this work, and which is usually offered in the initial periods of technology, computing and engineering courses, most students have greater difficulty in learning the initial concepts, such as logic, which then generates a high degree of reprovals and dropouts (PRIETCH and PAZETO, 2010). In addition, the fact that these subjects have cumulative contents, if the students do not dedicate themselves from the beginning, this increases the possibility that they cannot follow the course and therefore fail or give up (RAPOSO; DANTAS, 2016).

Still according to Raposo and Dantas (2016), teachers need to look for ways to awaken students' interest in programming subjects, making it possible for them to maintain a constant rhythm of studies. This goal can be achieved precisely by using information technology in education. However, Brito Junior (2016) points out that education professionals need to overcome major challenges regarding the use of these resources, such as, for example, the SEs, in traditional Brazilian education.

2.2. EDUCATIONAL *SOFTWARE*

An IF is a didactic-pedagogical resource with the purpose of helping the teaching-learning and that is used in the best way when there is the mediation of the teacher, being then a means of teaching (BRITO JUNIOR, 2016). This resource serves as a support not only for the student but also for the teacher. The process of adaptation of many people to such resources is a negative point, but the shortening of the learning curve and the greater range of information are positive aspects of SE, and therefore contribute positively to the learning process (PENHA, 2015).

One fact that attests to the advantage of using SE in education is that young people learn best when the environment is consistent with their daily lives (FIALHO; MATOS, 2010, p.123). However, for the SE to be truly effective, it must be easy to use, be able to sustain the user's attention and be of simple understanding, among other factors (TAVARES, 2017).

For *software to* be considered educational, it only needs to be inserted into the medium in question - as long as it meets the needs of the context - even if it was not designed with such an objective in mind (TEIXEIRA; BRANDÃO, 2003). In addition, Oliveira, Menezes and Moreira (2001) consider that those SE made with the specific objective of helping in the learning process are called educational *software*, which are a subgroup of the SE.

The SEs can also be classified according to their focus and usability, and can be exercise *software,* simulation software, applications, educational games, tutorials, programming language software and research software, such as dictionaries (TAVARES, 2017).

Below, the characteristics of each are described:

A. **Exercise *software*:** these are those that present questions and receive answers from users, evaluating their performance;

B. **Simulation software:** allow the student to participate in activities through real simulations;

C. **Applications:** are not developed for educational purposes, but can be used for that purpose;

D. **Educational games:** allow the user to learn in a playful and dynamic way;

E. **Tutorials:** are *software* that are taught through the presentation of information and instructions to the student;

F. **Programming language *softwares*:** they are those that allow the creation of new *software* without great programming knowledge;

G. **Investigation software:** *Software* that allows the user to find information, such as dictionaries.

In general, the SEs can be developed for numerous platforms according to the needs of the medium: *mobile*, *desktop* and *web*. The system of this work deals with a *web* platform.

2.3. ACADEMIC LOOP

The SE called *Loop Academic*, according to Souza, Dyego (2019), is a *web* platform still under development whose focus is to assist the teaching-learning process of the introductory programming courses in higher level courses, taking into account that most students in computer and related courses have difficulty in these disciplines. The system, which is under development, is composed of three modules: Student Module, aimed at students of introductory programming disciplines; Teacher Module, aimed at teachers of the same disciplines; and Monitor Module, aimed at programming monitors.

In the work done by Souza, Dyego (2019), the process of elicitation of requirements was executed from the application of *surveys* with beginner students in programming, the prototyping and, finally, the evaluation of the usability of the Student module; while this work deals with the development of the *front-end* of the same module.

2.4. *WEB* DEVELOPMENT

The Internet has expanded exponentially and this has a significant impact on several sectors, including education, and this popularization is due to the user's ease of obtaining access to information and creating content (GINIGE; MURUGESAN, 2001). A *web* system is characterized by the processing of the application taking place on a remote computer, called Server (MILLETO; BERTAGNOLLI, 2014, p. 4).

However, there are two stages of *web* development: the *front-end*, aimed at user interaction, where their processes are performed by the browser itself; and the *back-end*, where the processes are performed by the server. Each step requires different construction modes and languages.

From the analysis according to the criteria listed in chapter 4, HTML5 markup language, CSS style language and *JavaScript scripting language* were chosen, as well as the IDE (Integrated Development Environment) *Visual Studio Code* as development environment, the *Bootstrap framework* and the *jQuery library*, which will be detailed in the next subsections.

2.4.1. FRONT-END

As said before, the process of developing *web* pages or systems usually involves two phases: the *front-end* and the *back-end*. According to Fernandes (2017), the *front-end* is mainly focused on the part of the page interface, responsible for displaying and receiving information (which can be processed and stored through *back-end*), taking into consideration *Software* Engineering concepts such as usability. Furthermore, this axis, also called *Client-Side*, is interpreted directly in the user's browser, and this is a technical factor that differentiates it from the *Server-Side,* which runs on a server. As the *front-end* is mainly focused on graphic aspects, the main languages used in its development are those capable of handling interfaces, components, interactions and events of a *web* page, being

they HTML, CSS and *JavaScript*.

2.4.1.1 HTML

HyperText Markup Language (HTML), which is currently in version 5, is the standard language for creating *web* pages and describes the structure of *web* pages through the use of *tags,* which are elements that "inform" the browser how each piece of information should be displayed, for example, as paragraphs, links and headers (W3SCHOOLS, 2019a). Figure 1 represents a simple example of the use of HTML, where the instruction <! *DOCTYPE>* specifies to the browser the HTML version of the document, while the tags < head> *and*

< body> define the "head" and "body" of the page, respectively. The < title> *is* used to determine the title that is shown in a web browser tab, while the <h2> *and* <p> tags are text elements (header and paragraph), and must always be positioned within the < body>.

Figure 1: Example HTML document

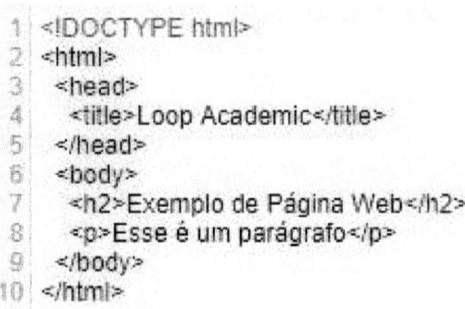

Source: Own author

A browser is capable of interpreting HTML code. Figure 2 shows the screen that is displayed by the *browser from* the code in Figure 1.

Figure 2 Result of the HTML excerpt of Figure 1

Source: Own author

According to Silva (2016), HTML appeared in the 90's as a document used to arrange the content on the browser screen, and in version 5, besides having good compatibility with old *browsers*, presented a series of features previously unavailable and that make the tool more powerful for building *web* pages. Below, some of these features are listed:

- Graphic elements: < canvas>, <svg>;
- Form attributes such as *date*, *number* and *range*;
- *Tags* of semantic elements, like < header> and < footer>.

2.4.1.2 CSS

From version 3.2 of HTML, some elements of content stylization were added to the language, and this generated a certain difficulty for developers due to the amount of information that should be added to each page, which made development slow and expensive. To solve this problem, the *World Wide Web Consortium* (W3C) developed a *Cascading Style Sheets (*CSS) language, whose function is to describe the form and style that HTML elements and content should be displayed on the browser screen (W3SCHOOLS, 2019b).

In general, the CSS, which is currently in version 3, is able to modify the colors and visual effects of *web* pages (SILVA, 2016), such as text color, font size, apply gradient effects, define margins and even create animations. The CSS can be written in three ways:

- **Inline** *Style*: that is, within a single element of the HTML document through the *style* attribute, modifying the attributes only of the *tag* to which it is inserted;

- **Internal Style Sheet**: also being written in the HTML document, but within the *style* tag, being able to modify the attributes of the entire page;

- **External Style Sheet**: written in an external file that contains only the CSS, this way it is possible to change the appearance of all the pages that refer to the style sheet.

Figure 3 exemplifies an excerpt from a style sheet, where the *background-color* property indicates the color of the "*body*" selector, which represents the same name *tag* of an HTML document. For the "p" selector, also referring to HTML, the *font-family* property determines the *font* type, while *font-size* defines the size of the *font* and *color*, its color.

Figure 3: Example external CSS style sheet

```
1  body {
2    background-color: lightgray;
3  }
4
5  p {
6    font-family: 'Times New Roman', Times, serif;
7    font-size: 16px;
8    color: brown;
9  }
```

Source: Own author

2.4.1.3 JAVASCRIPT

JavaScript is a multi-paradigmatic *scripting* language that can be interpreted or compiled *Just-in-Time* (JIT). Officially, its name is *ECMAScript*, but *Oracle*[2]'s trademark is *JavaScript* (MDN, 2019). It is interesting to note that although they have similar names, *Java* and *JavaScript* are totally different languages, both in syntax and application.

This language is of great importance for the *web* development process because it allows creating interactive pages that are not only possible with HTML and CSS when adding responses to DOM actions and events[3], among others.

---

[2] Link from Oracle's official website: https://www.oracle.com/index.html
[3] *Document Object Model*, is a document created by the browser that allows *JavaScript*

Moreover, according to a survey conducted in 2018 by *StackOverflow,* one of the largest question and answer sites focused on programming and development, *JavaScript* is the most popular language among professional developers, as shown in Chart 1. Chart 2 also shows that approximately 40 % of the developers participating in the survey work with the *front-end* and 50 % declare themselves *full-stack, that* is, they work with both the *front-end* and the *back-end*, significant numbers that may have influenced the high popularity of *JavaScript*.

Graph 1: List of the most popular languages among professional *StackOverflow* users

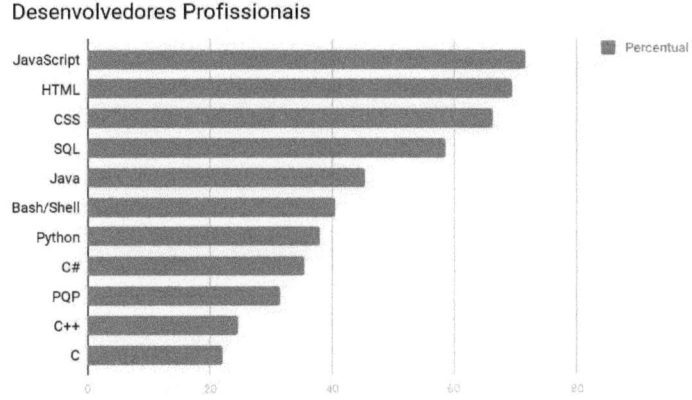

Source: Adapted from *StackOverflow* (2018)

access and manipulate each element of the HTML.

Graph 2: Types of *StackOverflow* developers users

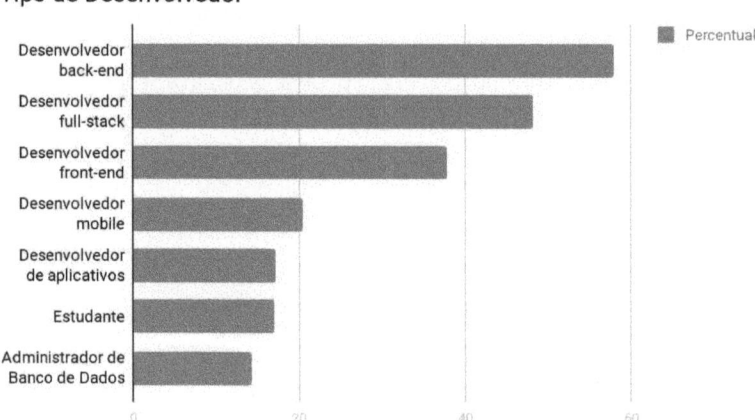

Source: Adapted from *StackOverflow* (2018)

In addition, *JavaScript* has a large number of external tools that can be used to increase the power of the language, such as *jQuery*.

2.4.1.4 BOOTSTRAP FRAMEWORK

The *Twitter Bootstrap framework*, whose version used in this research was the 4, is, according to the developers, a toolkit written in CSS and *JavaScript and* that has *plugins* built in *jQuery,* and allows to create responsive sites (not limited to that) through its grid system. [4]According to Balasubramanee et at. (2013, our translation):

> *Twitter Bootstrap* is a powerful *framework* that provides a set of CSS classes and JavaScript functions to facilitate the *front-end* development process. Its responsive *design* feature allows support for both *mobile* device screens and *desktop* computers [...].

It is important to note that this work does not focus on system responsiveness, since it was developed based on the prototype of the Student module, which in turn presents only the *web* version for *desktop*.

According to the developer's information, *Bootstrap*'s standard formatting for

---

[4] Taken from *Bootstrap*'s official website: https://getbootstrap.com

web pages is composed of containers in their outermost part, which in turn group rows and columns inside them, which can be specified through the use of *.container* or *.container-fluid*, *. row, .col* and their variations, which are predefined in *Bootstrap's* documentation and can be enabled in HTML elements such as div and nav (BOOTSTRAP, 2019). The structure behaves as shown in Figure 4, where the element with the

. container acts as a kind of container for the *.row* element, which functions as a row of a mathematical matrix, where elements with the *.col* class accommodate and act as columns.

Figure 4: Graphical representation of *Bootstrap* 4 grid system

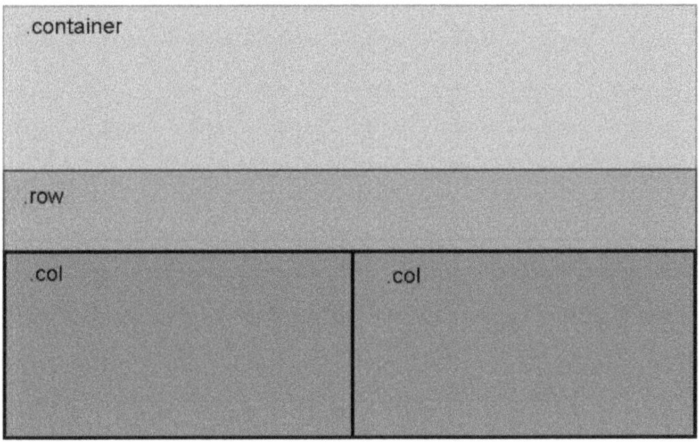

[figure: diagram showing .container containing .row containing two .col elements]

Source: Own author

2.4.1.5   *jQUERY*

Being classified as a *JavaScript library*, *jQuery* is versatile and lightweight. According to Silva (2016) and the developers themselves[5], this library allows the manipulation of HTML DOM, animations, events, CSS and AJAX[6] to be simplified in relation to pure *JavaScript* code, besides having compatibility with most browsers. The version used in this work was 3.3.1.

Figure 5 shows an example of *jQuery* application written *inline*, that is, inside the HTML file itself, where the first function activates the *modal* "*show*" attribute (*Bootstrap* element) as soon as the page is loaded, that is, it shows that element on the screen; the second function activates the "*hide*" attribute, which

---
[5] Link from *jQuery*'s official website: https://jquery.com
[6] It is a technique that makes use of *JavaScript* and the DOM to allow *web* pages to be updated asynchronously.

hides the same *modal* when receiving a click event on an element specified in the HTML.

Figure 5: Example of *JavaScript* code written through *jQuery* library

```
5  <script>
6      $(window).on('load', function()
7      {
8          $('#tela_validacao1').modal('show');
9      })
10     $(document).ready(function()
11     {
12         $('#validade_code1').click(function()
13         {
14             $('#tela_validacao1').modal('hide');
15         })
16     })
17 </script>
```

Source: Own author

3. RELATED WORKS

This chapter provides summaries of some scientific papers that are related to this research.

In the work presented by Souza, Cláudio (2016), the author states that there is a great difficulty on the part of the students in understanding the subjects of introductory programming, either for lack of preparation of the students or for lack of didactic resources that help the students and teachers. The author then presents a study on the implementation of VisuAlg, a program that simulates the traditional pseudocode through the so-called Portugol, but in a way that is closer to traditional programming languages and aims to assist both students and teachers in teaching and learning the programming disciplines, while making a comparison between the traditional teaching method and the new approaches. Finally, the article notes that the use of teaching aids should be used more widely and highlights that the use of VisuAlg in the early stages of programming has been productive and efficient in improving student learning, as it allows them to have closer contact with real programming environments.

Santos Sobrinha et al. (2016) deals with the development of an *Application Programming Interface* (API) developed in C++ and *Python*, aimed at communication and control of a teaching robot, in addition to the development of a Visual Programming Platform (PPV), whose focus is to make the process of learning programming more attractive both for beginners and for students who have some type of hearing impairment. In other words, the authors aim to use robotics and PPV to assist students in subjects such as programming and mathematics. In the course of their work, the authors present several examples of practical applications of both API and PPV and show how this type of tool can be useful to arouse more interest and facilitate the learning of students in the cited disciplines.

The authors Junior, Sandro and Souza (2014) seek to analyze how effective Object Oriented Programming (POO) teaching using the Rede Social Educativa - REDU - can be. For this purpose, samples were made through the students of the POO curricular component of the Degree in Computing. As results, the authors found that the use of this platform as an option of teaching methodology proved beneficial and was able to assist the teacher in the process of planning, teaching and evaluating the teaching of POO. Therefore, according to the work, the use of the social network in question in the academic environment is presented as a new option of teaching method where the teacher ceases to be just a transmitter of information and becomes a mediator.

The article presented by Camargo e Fortunato (2018) deals with a study on the use of the Scratch program applied to teaching-learning programming between 2010 and 2016. For this purpose, researches were conducted in the repository of the Coordination for the Improvement of Higher Level Personnel (CAPES) and the data obtained showed that the use of the *software has* increased a lot over the years, going from few researches in the area in 2010 to many in the period of 2016. The authors affirm, then, that this increase in interest in Scratch demonstrates that the tool is fulfilling its purpose of assisting in teaching and learning programming.

Chaves et al. (2014) is about MOJO, a tool that integrates both the *online* judges system and *Moodle*, which is a virtual learning environment; the idea of involving both systems started from the need for greater involvement of the programming teacher and the availability of more practical issues. This platform focuses on reducing the burden of tasks on the teacher from the automation of processes, where the teacher can manage the teaching resources and streamline the processes of preparation, submission and evaluation of activities. The results presented in this research show that most teachers agree that a platform like MOJO would be useful in reducing the time spent on corrections, submissions and elaboration of activities and that it would also be easier to follow up on students due to the reduction of the overload on teachers, in addition to being able to give faster *feedback* to the student.

4. METHODOLOGY

A series of procedures were used to carry out the proposed work. All these processes are described in this chapter and follow the structure presented in Figure 6.

Figure 6: Methodology for the development of the SE *front-end*

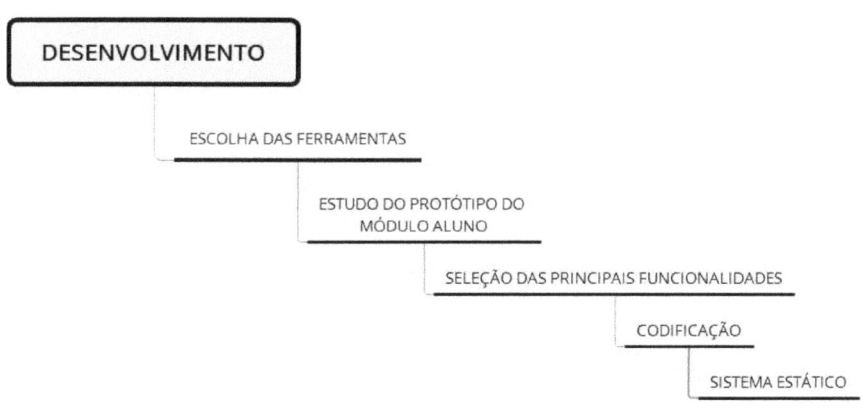

Source: Own author

4.1. CHOICE OF TOOLS

To develop a *software*, whatever it is, it is necessary to encode it using languages that can be interpreted or compiled, which can be programming, *scripting* or even markup and style - the latter aimed at the *web* universe. For this, a simple text editor can be used to write such code, however, there are tools called IDEs that add other features and resources capable of increasing developer productivity, among other factors.

In order to select the most appropriate languages for this work, technical criteria were taken into consideration, according to the model presented in Sebesta (2015), summarized in Table 1, which, despite having a focus on programming languages, were also applied in this work to markup and style languages due to the fact that there is no consolidated metric or criteria for the evaluation of *front-end languages*. In addition, the general criteria shown in Table 3 were also used: Learning curve, Relevance in the current market and Portability. For the IDEs, the resources available among some models, being ATOM, *Visual Studio Code* and *NetBeans*, were compared in order to find the most appropriate for the needs of this search.

Table 1. Technical criteria for evaluating languages and the characteristics that affect them

Feature	CRITERION		
	LEGIBILITY	WRITING FACILITY	RELIABILITY
Simplicity	✓ ✓	✓ ✓	✓ ✓
Orthogonality	✓	✓ ✓ ✓	✓
Types of Data	✓	✓ ✓ ✓	✓
Syntax *Design*	✓	✓ ✓ ✓	✓
Abstraction support		✓	✓ ✓ ✓
Expressiveness		✓	✓ ✓ ✓
Type Check			✓ ✓
Handling Exceptions			✓ ✓
Restricted *Aliasing*			✓ ✓

Source: Adapted from Sebesta (2015)

According to Sebesta (2015), the readability criterion is characterized, among other factors, by the ease of understanding the code, the amount of writing resources available and the orthogonality. Ease of writing is a criterion that varies a lot according to the *software,* because, for example, systems that need deeper access to memory management will need to use lower level languages; however, this criterion is also related to readability and the amount of writing resources. Finally, reliability is closely related to the security and error checking that the language offers.

Based on the analysis of the technical criteria in Table 1, the HTML, CSS and *JavaScript* languages were evaluated, according to Table 2.

Table 2. Evaluation of HTML, CSS and *JavaScript* languages: technical criteria

Critérios→	LEGIBILITY			WRITING FACILITY			RELIABILITY		
Languages ↓	Download	Average	Top	Download	Average	Top	Download	Average	Top
HTML		✓			✓		Does not apply		
CSS		✓			✓		Does not apply		
JavaScript		✓			✓			✓	

Source: Own author

Since HTML and CSS are not programming languages and only deal with the visual part of the elements of a *web* page, the reliability criteria does not apply to them.

Table 3 presents the evaluation of languages based on the three general criteria cited, which refer to the needs of the work itself and the author, as time available for developing this research.

Table 3. Evaluation of HTML, CSS and *JavaScript* languages: general criteria

Critérios→	Learning Curve			Relevance			Portability		
Languages ↓	Download	Average	Top	Download	Average	Top	Download	Average	Top
HTML	✓				✓				✓
CSS	✓				✓				✓
JavaScript	✓	✓			✓✓				✓✓

Source: Own author

HTML and CSS languages are relatively easy to learn when compared to other types of languages, such as programming. For this reason their learning curve is low, whereas *JavaScript* requires a little more study of syntax and its operation, which results in an average curve. When it comes to relevance, that is, how important these languages are in the current market, all of them have shown a high relevance, according to Chart 1. Portability, on the other hand, which is related to how well a language can be applied in different architectures, presents a high value for all evaluated languages, since they are focused on the *web*, present high compatibility with the main browsers on the market and can be used regardless of the machine architecture and its Operating System (OS).

Next, a review of the features and functionalities of three of the main IDEs available and used for *web* development, *Visual Studio Code,* ATOM and *Netbeans*, was performed in order to choose the one that best fits the needs of this work. In Table 4, the main resources of these tools are available.

Table 4. Main features of some *web* development IDEs

ATOM	**Visual Studio Code**	**Netbeans**
OpenSource	*OpenSource*	*OpenSource*
Multiplatform	Multiplatform	Multiplatform
Highly customizable	Take	It has code *templates*
Able to work with numerous projects at once	Extensions for several languages	Able to work with numerous projects at once
Assists text editing processes	Several *debugging* options	Support of *plug-ins* for several languages
	IntelliSense: help system to autocomplete words	Assists text editing processes

Source: Own author

Note that all development environments mentioned in Table 4 have similar features, however, *Visual Studio Code* stands out for its high performance and ability to easily work with numerous languages and projects at once, providing a complete environment for *web* development, which requires parallel coding of HTML, CSS and *JavaScript* to generate good results.

When it comes to *Frameworks* and *Libraries, Bootstrap* has proved to be very useful due to its high capacity to provide the customization of *web* pages by using containers, columns and rows to split the *browser* screen, while facilitating responsiveness, as explained in section 2.3.5. For these reasons, *Bootstrap* was chosen as one of the tools to aid development. In addition, *jQuery,* which has already been discussed in section 2.3.6, has also been adopted for simplifying *JavaScript* itself, with easy handling of events and the DOM.

4.2. STUDY OF THE STUDENT MODULE PROTOTYPE

According to Souza, Dyego (2019), the *Loop Academic* system should have three modules when it is finished: Student, Teacher and Monitor. This step consists in the analysis of the requirements and functionalities present in the prototype of the Student module developed in the previous work, as already mentioned, in order to list them. Due to this, the study of the prototype and its documentation was carried out in order to make a survey of all the requirements present in the module in question, based on the diagram of Use Cases presented by Souza, Dyego (2019).

Below are listed all the functional requirements of the Student module.

- Register as a Student;
- Login;
- Solve Exercise;
- See Support Code;
- See Support Material;
- See Tips;
- See Performance;
- Send Questions;
- Create Forum Topic;
- Answer Forum Topic;
- See Emblems.

4.3. SELECTION OF MAIN FUNCTIONALITIES

Based on the survey of requirements and the time available to perform the work in question, only those functionalities judged to be the main ones were chosen to be developed, where those listed with Essential priority in the requirements document, made by Souza, Dyego (2019), were selected, as well as some marked with Important priority, which, in turn, do not require the *back-end* directly and are basic for the initial operation of the system. The main features selected are listed below:

- Register as a Student;
- Login;
- Solve Exercise;
- See Support Code;
- See Support Material;
- See Tips;
- See Performance;
- See Emblems.

The requirements related to the forum and the doubts were not prioritized by the fact that they require, in a more intense way, the *back-end,* therefore, it was understood by the authors that it is more interesting that these functionalities are done in the future with the *front-end* together with the *back-end*.

Each functionality listed has internal actions that can be classified as main flow, alternative and exception flows, such as invalid code functions, return, cancel and save, according to the Student module prototype.

4.4. CODIFICATION

After the selection of languages, tools and functionalities, the process of coding the functional requirements *front-end* was started, as well as its main, alternative and exception flows from the system *front-end,* characterized by the use of HTML, CSS, *JavaScript* and external tools to shape the platform based on the already existing interface prototype. For that, HTML was used to define the structure of each page, with its sections, headers, etc, besides CSS together with *Bootstrap,* to stylize and customize each HTML document. In addition, *JavaScript* and *jQuery* were responsible for manipulating the system's actions, as well as handling events such as clicking, page loading, among others.

At the end of the *front-end* coding a static system is developed, that is, the user is not able to store data and information in it, a process that will be possible after the development and implementation of the *back-end* in future works.

5. RESULTS AND DISCUSSIONS

This chapter presents the results obtained from the development of the *Loop Academic* Student module *front-end*, as well as a brief discussion about them.

5.1. FRONT-END DEVELOPMENT

As highlighted in the previous chapters, HTML was used to structure static pages, CSS to stylize them and, finally, *JavaScript* to help the interaction between the user and the system and manipulate the behavior of the pages.

The first part of the system consists in the implementation of the registration and *login* requirements, as shown in Figure 7. It is important to emphasize that, because this work focuses on the implementation of the *front-end*, therefore there is no validation of data entered in any of the fields of registration or *login*, because for this to occur, it is necessary that the *back-end* is implemented, allowing *link* the system to a database.

Figure 7. Initial screen of *Loop Academic*

Source: Own author

For this purpose, the structure present in Figure 8 was built using *Bootstrap* elements to organize the document in rows and columns. The internal sections containing text and form were omitted with the intention of simplifying the reading of the code. Because it has no *back-end*, the action of the form is just to redirect the welcome screen. The ids and classes are used to allow the CSS to modify specific HTML selectors, as shown in Figure 9.

Figure 8. HTML excerpt from the home page

```
1  <body style="background-color: rgb(28, 118, 134)">
2      <div class="container">
3          <div class="row justify-content-center">
4              <div class="col-10 col-md-4" id="login_screen">
5                  ...
6              </div>
7          </div>
8          <div class="row justify-content-center">
9              <div class="col-10 col-md-4" id="login_box">
10                 <form action="boas_vindas.html">
11                     ...
12                 </form>
13             </div>
14         </div>
15         <div class="row justify-content-center">
16             <div class="col-10 col-md-4" id="bottom_box">
17                 ...
18             </div>
19         </div>
20         <div class="row justify-content-center">
21             <div class="col-10 col-md-4" id="sign_up_box">
22                 ...
23             </div>
24         </div>
25     </div>
26 </body>
```

Source: Own author

Figure 9. Excerpt from the CSS referring to the home page

```
1  #login_screen {
2      margin-top: 10%;
3      background-color: white;
4      min-height: 80px;
5      border-style: double;
6      border-color: white;
7      border-top-left-radius: 5px;
8      border-top-right-radius: 5px;
9  }
10 #login_box {
11     background-color: rgb(240, 240, 240);
12     padding-left: 0.5%;
13     padding-top: 2%;
```

Source: Own author

By clicking "Create my account", the user is redirected to a user profile selection menu, which allows him to inform whether he wants to register as a student, teacher or monitor, as shown in Figure 10. The options "Teacher" and "Monitor" refer to the modules that will be developed in the future, that is, the complete documentation or the prototype of these modules has not yet been done, according to Souza, Dyego (2019).

Figure 10. User Profiles

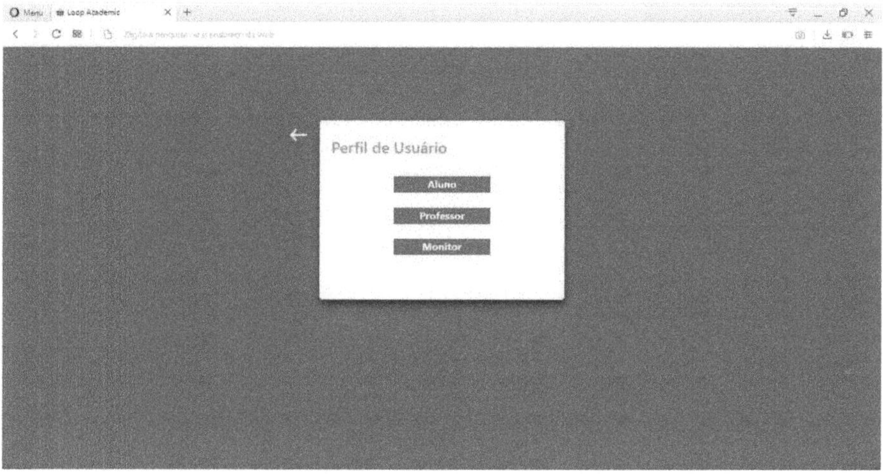

Source: Own author

By selecting the "Student" option, a registration form is displayed, as shown in Figure 11, which allows the student to create their account on the system. After having a registered account, the student will be able to *login* through the system's initial screen according to Figure 7, and then will come across a welcome screen, (Figure 12), where the student will be required to enter his/her Virtual Class code, which code should be released by the teacher himself/herself after he/she registers a Virtual Class in the system (functionality not yet available in this work).

Figure 11. Student Registration - *Loop Academic*

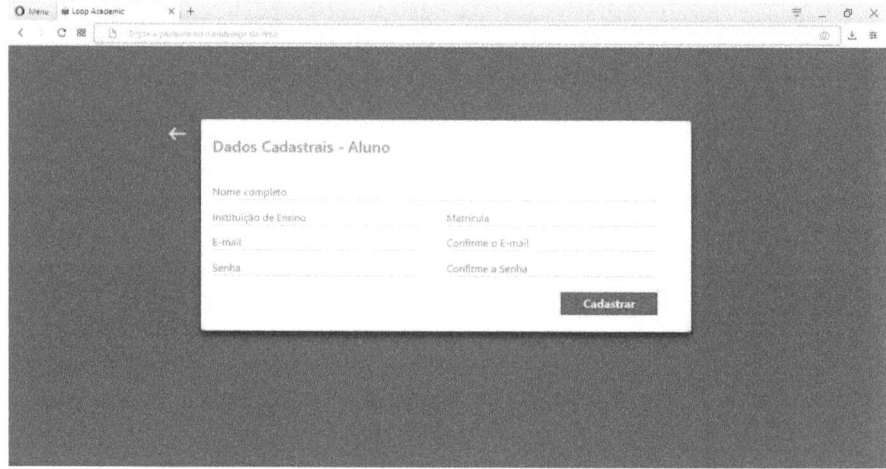

Source: Own author

Figure 12. Welcome screen

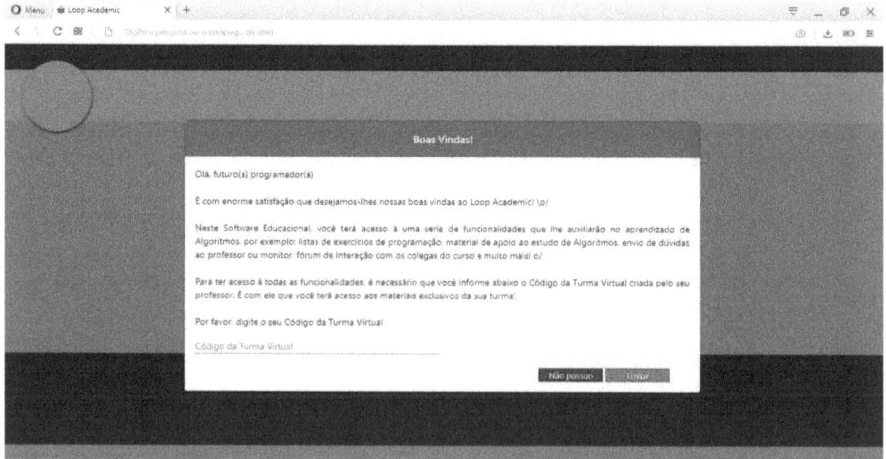

Source: Own author

The welcome screen was conceived through the use of *modal*, which is a *Bootstrap plugin* built in CSS and *JavaScript* (*jQuery*) applied to HTML. Figure 13 shows the structure used by the author, with *inline* CSS, to develop the screen of Figure 12. In addition, the *jQuery* code presented in Figure 5 was also applied to the HTML document to control when the *modal* should be displayed or hidden.

Figure 13. HTML - *Bootstrap Modal*

```
1   <div class="row">
2    <div class="col-12">
3     <!-- Modal 1 -->
4     <div class="modal fade" id="tela_validacao1" tabindex="-1" data-backdrop="static" data-
          keyboard="false" role="dialog" aria-labelledby="myModalTitle" aria-hidden="true">
5      <div class="modal-dialog modal-dialog-centered modal-lg" role="document">
6       <div class="modal-content">
7        <div class="modal-header">
8         <div style="width: 100%; text-align: center;">
9          ...
10        </div>
11       </div>
12       <div class="modal-body" style="font-size: 14px;">
13        <div class="row">
14         <div class="col-12" style="text-align: justify;">
15          ...
16         </div>
17        </div>
18        <input type="text" name="codigo_virtual" id="virtual_code" placeholder="Código da
           Turma Virtual">
19        <br>
20        <div class="row justify-content-end">
21         <div class="col-4">
22          <br>
23          <button type="button" data-toggle="modal" data-target="#tela_validacao2"
            id="validate_code1">Não possuo</button>
24          <input type="submit" value="Enviar" onclick="validate_input('virtual_code')"
            id="validate_code2">
25         </div>
26        </div>
27       </div>
28      </div>
29     </div>
30    </div>
31   </div>
32  </div>
```

Source: Own author

Once again, because it is only the *front-end,* the validation of the code is only symbolic and performed by the *validate_input*() function, imported from the *JavaScript script*, (Figure 14), which performs the conditional test for user input and redirects it to an invalid code screen if nothing is entered or to a valid code screen if any data is entered.

Figure 14. Function of *JavaScript*

```
1  function validate_input(id) {
2      var value_input = document.getElementById(id).value;
3      if (value_input == "")
4      {
5          window.location.href = "codigo_invalido.html";
6      }
7      else
8      {
9          window.location.href = "codigo_valido.html";
10     }
11 }
12
```

Source: Own author

Having the code validated, if so, the student is redirected to the main menu, shown in Figure 15, otherwise the system activates the exception flow, notifies the user that the code is invalid and offers the option to insert it again or return to the initial screen. The main menu, as well as all the other functionalities implemented, were developed using the grid structure, already mentioned and shown, of *Bootstrap*.

Figure 15. *Loop Academic* Main Menu

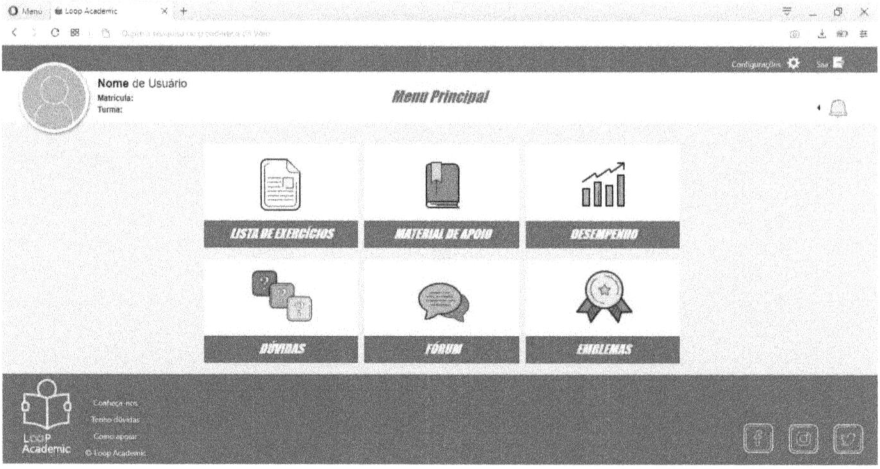

Source: Own author

When accessing the main menu, the student can choose from one of six options, in this case, the Exercise List, Support Materials, Performance and Emblems menus are available.

When choosing the Exercise List option, the student has access to all the available exercises and can select which one they wish to answer, as shown in Figure 16. When selecting one of the exercises, Figure 17 is displayed, in which there is the possibility of the user writing and executing the code on the system itself through the Repl.it compiler[7] embedded in the page.

Figure 16. List of Exercises

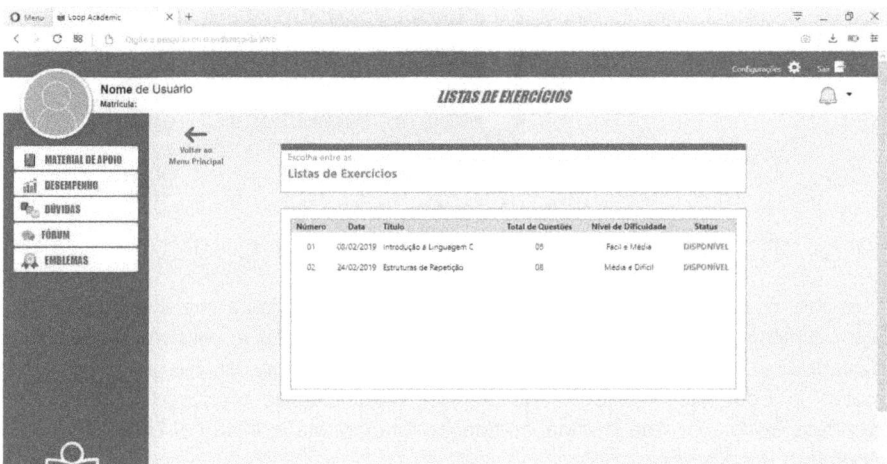

Source: Own author

The user can then write their code and run it directly from the browser through the *online* compiler cited, and see their *output*. There are also options to save the code to respond later or send to the teacher to fix, however, they will only be effectively implemented after the development of the *back-end*. The "Tips" and "Support Code" tabs are controlled via *Bootstrap modal* and display help content for each question. The "Support Material" tab redirects the user to the menu with the same name, according to Figure 18.

---

[7] Repl.it homepage: https://repl.it

Figure 17. Exercise List

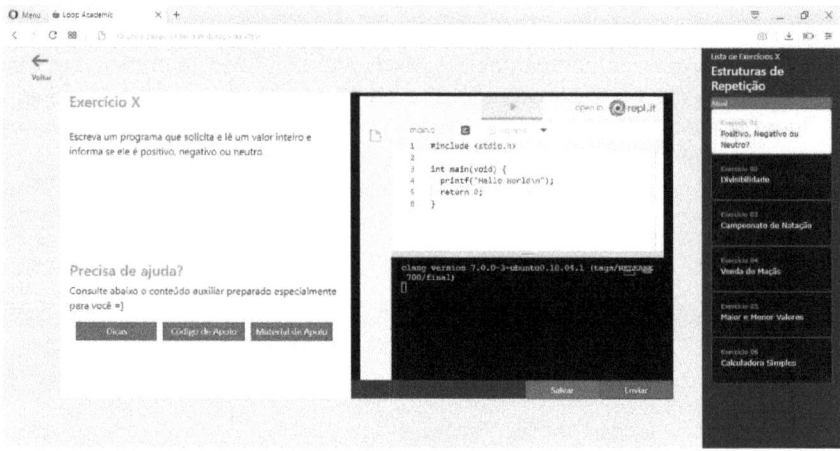

Source: Own author

In the Support Material menu, (Figure 18), the available materials are displayed, which are unlocked as they are viewed. The materials accessible inside the system are composed by productions of the Laboratory of Research in Informatics in Education - LABIE, and also by video classes produced by the *Programming Loop*, *Youtube* channel composed by students/monitors of UFERSA - Campus Pau dos Ferros.

Figure 18. Support Material

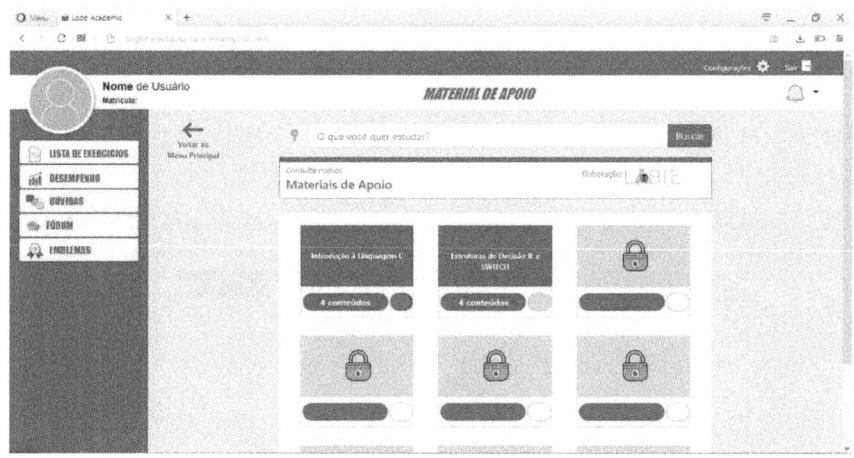

Source: Own author

Through *onclick* events, *JavaScript*, written *inline*, is able to make the page display a message of blocked content when the user clicks *on* one of the materials not yet accessible, according to the code in Figure 19.

Figure 19. Events controlled via *JavaScript*

```
1   <div class="col col_content">
2     <div class="content_section" style="background-color: lightblue;">
3       <p><b><!--CONTEÚDO BLOQUEADO--></b></p>
4       <img class="content_blocked" src="Images/Conteúdo bloqueado.png">
5       <div class="button_box" style="background-color: white;">
6         <div>
7           <button class="conteudos" onclick="window.alert('Conteúdo bloqueado! ();"
              onmouseover="new_color(this)" onmouseout="old_color(this)"></button>
8         </div>
9         <div class="circle" style="background-color: white;"></div>
10      </div>
11    </div>
12  </div>
```

Source: Own author

Figure 20 shows one of the support materials, composed of the *Programming Loop* channel video lessons embedded in the page. The side menu specifies which material is currently being displayed and allows the user to select them freely, while the "Previous" and "Next" buttons allow navigation between the contents. Both functions are controlled via *JavaScript,* while part of the style is left to the standard *Bootstrap* classes, as shown in Figure 21.

Figure 20. Example of Support Material

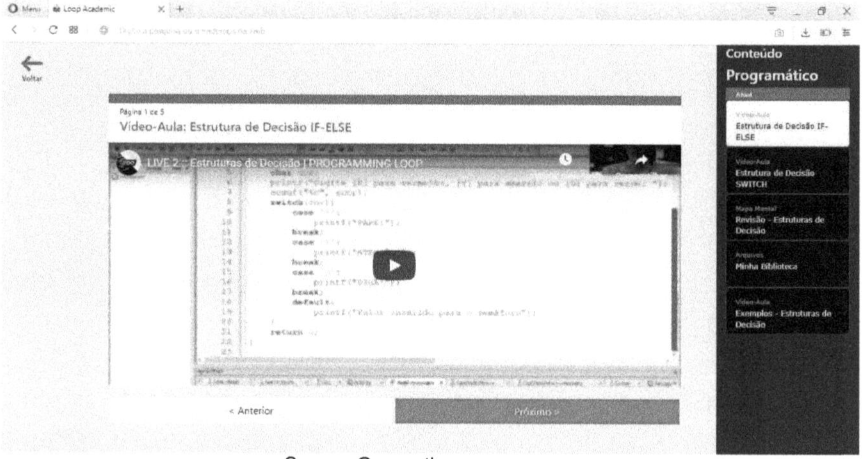

Source: Own author

Figure 21. HTML for Support Material

```
1   <div class="row justify-content-center">
2     <section class="col-11" style="margin-top: 8%;">
3       <div id="top_info">
4         <span>Página 1 de 5</span>
5         <h5>Vídeo-Aula: Estrutura de Decisão IF-ELSE</h5>
6       </div>
7       <div class="embed-responsive embed-responsive-21by9">
8         <iframe class="embed-responsive-item" src="https://www.youtube.com/embed/U8ixPxL54Sk"
                frameborder="0" allow="accelerometer; autoplay; encrypted-media; gyroscope; picture-in-picture"
                allowfullscreen></iframe>
9       </div>
10      <button class="back btn-light" type="button" disabled>< Anterior</button>
11      <button class="next" onclick="window.location.href='material_2.html';" type="button">Próximo >
        </button>
12    </section>
13  </div>
```

Source: Own author

The HTML code used to structure the page of Figure 20 can be found in Appendix A.

To represent how the badges obtained by the student will be displayed in the *Loop Academic*, it was chosen to represent some of them as if they had already been conquered (those that are not opaque) only in an illustrative way in Figure 22.

Figure 22. Emblem Screen

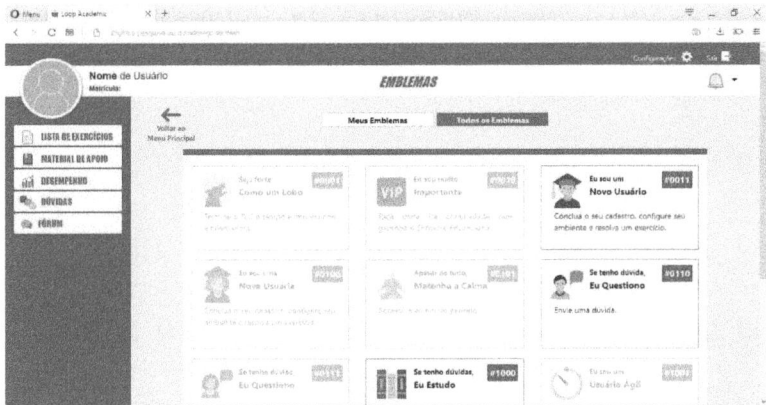

Source: Own author

Finally, Figure 23 displays the User Performance screen, where information regarding each exercise list is shown, as well as the percentage of hits and study recommendations if the student's performance was not satisfactory.

43

Figure 23. Performance Screen

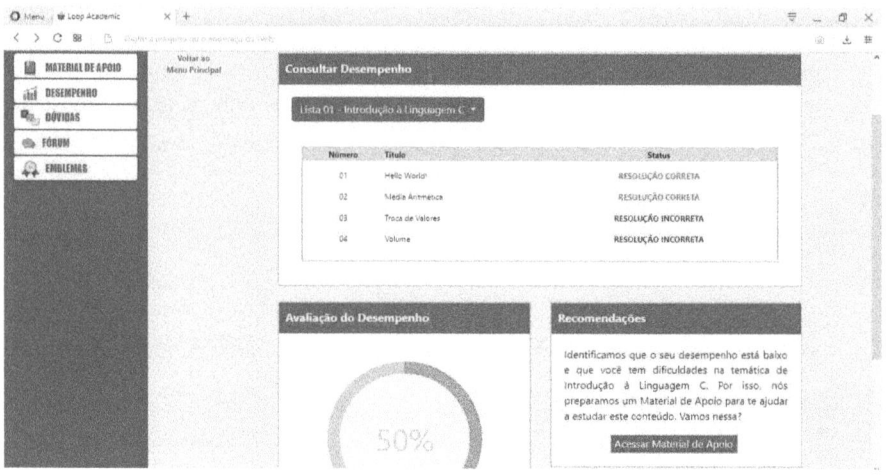

Source: Own author

In all pages of *Loop Academic*, *Bootstrap* was used to facilitate the configuration of the HTML elements and their layout on the screen, in order to leave the system as close as possible to the existing interface prototype. The *jQuery* was requested only in some moments when the events concerning some elements of *Bootstrap* required complementary actions, as in the case of the *modal* display when opening the system's welcome page.

6. FINAL CONSIDERATIONS

This work presented the development of the SE *Loop Academic front-end*, which aims to assist the teaching-learning process and reduce the difficulties that most students of the introductory programming disciplines have. With this, the *front-end* regarding the main functionalities of the Student module was developed using several *web* development tools and following the parameters defined through the study carried out previously, as already mentioned in the text, in which the prototype of the *web* platform in question was built based on the premises of Software Engineering.

From the results obtained, it can be seen that the main functionalities of the *client-side* of the Student module have been successfully implemented, from the point of view of coding the screens as presented in the prototype; and that the tools chosen have benefited the development of SE, because the current versions of HTML and CSS are powerful for creating *web* pages, in addition to *JavaScript*, which is able to manipulate elements of HTML in order to ensure greater dynamics to the system. In addition, *Visual Studio Code* proved to be very effective for *web* development and the chosen *framework* and *library* proved to be extremely effective, improving both productivity and page customization capabilities, especially *Bootstrap*, which was used throughout the project.

However, it is necessary that future work contemplates not only the two requirements not yet produced (Forum and Doubts), but also the *server-side* of the system. In addition, it is also noticeable that the two still undocumented modules, Professor and Monitor, need complete studies that start from the elicitation of functional and non-functional requirements to prototyping and, finally, the development of both the *front-end* and *back-end* for the *Loop Academic to* be fully developed.

7. REFERENCES

BALASUBRAMANEE, Viknes et al. Twitter bootstrap and AngularJS: Frontend frameworks to expedite science gateway development. **2013 IEEE International Conference On Cluster Computing (cluster)**, [s.l.], set. 2013. IEEE. http://dx.doi.org/10.1109/cluster.2013.6702640.

BOOTSTRAP. **Introduction**. Available in:

< https://getbootstrap.com/docs/4.3/getting-started/introduction/>. Access on June 29, 2019.

BRITO JUNIOR, Ozonias de Oliveira. **Approaches for evaluating educational software and its consistency with software quality models**. Master's Dissertation. Universidade Federal da Paraíba - UFPB/PPGI, João Pessoa - PB, 2016.

CALLAHAN, D., PEDIGO, B. **Educating Experienced IT Professionals by Addressing Industry's Needs**. IEEE Software, 2002, v. 19(5), p. 57-62.

CAMARGO, Ivan Rodrigues de; FORTUNATO, Ivan. Scratch as an aid in the process of teaching and learning programming language: a review of the national graduate program between 2010 and 2016. **Revista on line de Política e Gestão Educacional**, [S.l.], p. 608-626, may 2018. ISSN

1519-9029. Available in:

< https://periodicos.fclar.unesp.br/rpge/article/view/10754/7621>. Access on: 30 june 2019. doi:https://doi.org/10.22633/rpge.v22.n2.maio/ago.2018.10754.

CARITÁ, E.; SANCHES, L. M. P.; PADOVAN, V. Use of social networks in the teaching-learning process. In: **17th INTERNATIONAL CONGRESS OF EDUCATION TO DISTANCE**, 2011, Manaus.

CASPERSEN, Michael; KOLLING, Michael. Stream: A first programming process. **ACM Transactions on Computing Education**, Nova York, EUA, v. 9, n. 1, Article 4, 2009.

CHAVES, José Osvaldo Mesquita et al. MOJO: A TOOL TO INTEGRATE JUDGES ONLINE TO MOODLE IN SUPPORT OF PROGRAMMING TEACHING AND LEARNING. **Holos**, [l.s.], v. 5, n. , p.246-251, 30

Sept. 2014. Federal Institute of Education, Science and Technology of Rio Grande do Norte (IFRN). http://dx.doi.org/10.15628/holos.2014.1904.

DIOGINIS, Maria Lucineide et al. The new technologies in the teaching learning process. **Colloquium Humanarum**, Presidente Prudente, v. 12, n.

Special, p.1155-1162, October 2015. Quarterly. Available in:

≤ http://www.unoeste.br/site/enepe/2015/suplementos/area/Humanarum/Educ action/AS%20NEWS%20TECHNOLOGIES%20NO%20PROCESS%20DE% 2 0ENSINO%20APRENDIZAGEM.pdf>. Access on: 29 Jun. 2019.

FERNANDES, Tales Pinheiro. **Initial proposal of a *front-end web* development process using *web components*.** 2017. 64 f. TCC (Undergraduation) - Computer Science Course, Science Center

Tecnológicas, Universidade Estadual do Norte do Paraná, Bandeirantes, 2017.

FIALHO, Neusa; MATOS, Elizete. **The art of involving the student in the learning of**

sciences using educational software. Educar em Revista, Curitiba, n.

special 2, p. 121-136, 2010. UFPR Publisher. Available in:

< http://www.scielo.br/pdf/er/nspe2/07.pdf> Access on: 03 May 2019.

GOMES, Anabela de Jesus Gomes. **Difficulties in learning computer programming**: contributions to its understanding and resolution. PhD Thesis. University of Coimbra - UC/Computer Engineering Department, Coimbra - Portugal, 2010.

HOLANDA, Wallace, et al. **Challenges in learning introductory programming in IT courses at UFERSA, Pau dos Ferros campus**: an exploratory study. ECOP 2018, 19 to 21 March 2018, Pau dos Ferros, RN - ISSN 2526-7574 - v. 2, p. 90-96. Available in:

< https://periodicos.ufersa.edu.br/index.php/ecop>. Access on: May 04, 2019

GINIGE, A., MURUGESAN, S. **Web Engineering: an Introduction**, IEEE Multimedia, v. 8, n. 1, 2001, p. 14-18.

JUCÁ, Sandro C. Silveira. The relevance of educational software in professional education. **Revista Ciências e Cognição**, Rio de Janeiro, v. 8, 2006. Available in:

< http://www.cienciasecognicao.org/revista/index.php/cec/article/view/571/359

>. Access on: May 03, 2019.

JUNIOR, Elias Vidal Bezerra; SANDRO, Gomes Alex; SOUZA, Flavia Veloso Costa. **Analysis of teaching practice in the process of object oriented programming mediated by means of an educational social network**. EaD & Tecnologias Digitais na Educação, Dourados, v. 2, n. 3, p. 111-115, Nov. 2014. ISSN 2318-4051. Available in:

< http://ojs.ufgd.edu.br/index.php/ead/article/view/3414/2105>. Access on: 30 jun. 2019.

KOCH, Marlene Zimmermann. **Technologies in everyday school life: a facilitating tool in the teaching-learning process.** 2013. 36 f. Monograph (Specialization) - Educational Management Course, Postgraduate Center A Distância, Federal University of Santa Maria, Sarandi, 2013. Available in:

< https://repositorio.ufsm.br/bitstream/handle/1/498/Koch_Marlene_Zimmermann.pdf?sequence=1>. Access on: 29 jun. 2019.

Koile, K., & Singer, D. (2006). Improving learning in CS1 via tablet-PC-based- in-class assestment. **ICER 06: Proceedings of the Second International Workshop on Computing Education Research**. p. 119-126. ACM; Canterbury, UK.

LIMA, M. M. de; LIMA, A. R. de; MONTEIRO, A. C. C.; JÚNIOR, E. H. C..;

GOMES, L. d. Q. L. A Systematic Review of the Literature of Educational Software Development Processes. In: **Proceedings of the Brazilian Symposium of Informatics in Education**. [S.l.: n.], 2012. v. 23, n. 1.

MDN, Web Docs - Mozilla. **JAVASCRIPT BASICS**. 2019. Available in:

< https://developer.mozilla.org/en-US/docs/Learn/Getting_started_with_the_we b/JavaScript_basics>. Access on June 30, 2019.

MARKET, L. P. L. **New technologies in education**: Reflections on practice. Ed. UFAL, Maceió, 2002.

MILLETO, Evandro Manara; BERTAGNOLLI, Silvia de Castro. **Software Development II**: Introduction to *web* development with HTML, CSS, JavaScript and PHP. Rio Grande do Sul: bookman, 2014.

MORAN, José Manuel et al. **New Technologies and pedagogical mediation.**

6. Ed. Campinas; Papirus, 2000.

OLIVEIRA, C. C., Menezes, E. I., Moreira, M. **Ambiente Informativos de Aprendizagem**: production and evaluation of educational software.

Campinas: Papirus Publishing Company. 2001.

PEN, Daniel. **Educational Software for the Teaching-Learning of the 2nd Degree Equation**: Development and Evaluation. Lavras - MG, 2015.

Available at:< http://repositorio.ufla.br/jspui/handle/1/5249>. Access in: May 03, 2019.

Prietch, S. S., & Pazeto, T. A. **Study on Evasion in a Degree Course in Informatics and Considerations for Improvement.** WEIBASE, Maceió/AL. 2010.

RAPOSO, E. H. S.; DANTAS, V. The Snake Challenge - Using gamification to motivate students in an introductory programming course. **Annals of the XXVII Brazilian Symposium on Informatics in Education (SBIE 2016)**, [s.l.], v. 5, n. 27, p.577-586, 7 nov. 2016. Brazilian Computer Society - SBC.

SANTOS, Maria Adélia Icó dos. **Using Augmented Reality in Educational Software Development: an example in some concepts in Astronomy.** 2015. 106 f. Dissertation (Master's Degree) - Postgraduate Program in Applied Computing, Universidade Estadual de Feira de Santana, Feira de Santana - Ba, 2015. Available in:

< http://tede2.uefs.br:8080/handle/tede/366>. Access on: June 30, 2019.

SANTOS SOBRINHA, Vitória Heliane Pereira et al. Platform for Teaching Programming and Pedagogical Robotics. **Principia Magazine - Scientific and Technological Promotion of IFPB**, [S.l.], n. 31, p. 104-112, dec. 2016. ISSN 2447-9187. Available in:

< http://periodicos.ifpb.edu.br/index.php/principia/article/view/727>. Access on: 29 Jun. 2019.

doi:http://dx.doi.org/10.18265/1517-03062015v1n31p104-112.

SEBESTA, Robert W. **Concepts of Programming Languages**, 10ª ed. Pearson, 2015.

SILVA, FS., SERAPHIM, ML. Social networks in the teaching and learning process: with the word the adolescent. In: **SOUSA, RP., et al., eds. Theories and practices in educational technologies [online]**. Campina Grande: EDUEPB, 2016, p. 67-98. ISBN 978-85-7879-326-5. Available at:

< http://books.scielo.org/id/fp86k/pdf/sousa-9788578793265-04.pdf>. Access on: May 05, 2019.

SILVA, Gabriel Dumont de Lima e. **Development of a web system for food delivery order management in Diamantina/MG.** 2016. 76 f. TCC

(Graduate) - Information Systems Course, Faculty of Exact Sciences, Federal University of Jequitinhonha and Mucuri Valleys, Diamantina - Mg, 2016.

SOARES, Felipe A. L.; CARVALHO, Rodrigo B. de. **Proposal of an Educational Portal for Computer Programming Students.**

ABAKÓS, Institute of Exact Sciences and Informatics. PUC-Minas, 2017.

Available in:

< http://periodicos.pucminas.br/index.php/abakos/article/view/P.2316-9451.201 7v5n2p36/11700>. Access on: May 04, 2019.

SOUZA, Cláudio Morgado de. VisuAlg - Support Tool for Teaching Programming. **Teccen Electronic Magazine**, [s.l.], v. 2, n. 2, p.01-2, 3 oct.

2016. Half-yearly. Severino Sombra University.

http://dx.doi.org/10.21727/teccen.v2i2.234. Available at:

< http://editora.universidadedevassouras.edu.br/index.php/TECCEN/article/view/234>. Access on: 04 Jul. 2019.

SOUZA, Dyego Magno Oliveira. **Development and evaluation of the prototype of *Loop Academic*:** An Educational *Software* to assist in the teaching-learning process of introductory programming. 2019. 98 f. TCC (Graduation) - Information Technology Course, Universidade Federal Rural do Semi-Arido, Pau dos Ferros, 2019.

STACKOVERFLOW. **Developer Survey Results 2018.** Available in:

< https://insights.stackoverflow.com/survey/2018/>. Access on June 30, 2019.

TAVARES, Jéssika Lima. **Models, Techniques and Instruments of Educational Software Analysis**. UFPB. End of Course Work, 2017.

Available in:

< https://repositorio.ufpb.br/jspui/bitstream/123456789/2563/1/JLT19062017.pdf>. Access on: May 04, 2019.

TEIXEIRA, Adriano; BRANDÃO, Edemilson. Educational software: difficult start. **New Technologies in Education Magazine** - RENOTE. v. 1, n. 1.

CINTED/UFRGS, Feb. 2003. Available in:

< https://seer.ufrgs.br/renote/article/view/13629/7699>. Access on: May 04, 2019.

VALENTE, J. Armando. Communication and Education based on the use of Digital Information and Communication Technologies. **Revista UNIFESO**. v. 1, n. 1, 2014, p. 141-166.

W3Schools. **HTML INTRODUCTION.** Available in:

< https://www.w3schools.com/html/html_intro.asp>. Access on: June 30, 2019.

W3Schools. **CSS INTRODUCTION.** Available in:

< https://www.w3schools.com/css/css_intro.asp>. Access on: June 30, 2019.

8. ANNEX A - HTML Code

It has the HTML code used for coding the structure of the *web* page shown in Figure 20. In it, several language elements are used, such as the <div>, < button>, *<nav>* and <ul> *tags, as* well as *snippets* of inline CSS and standard *Bootstrap* classes, such as sidebar, *which* was *incorporated into* a <nav> tag to create a side menu.

```
<DOCTYPE html>
<html lang="pt-br">
  <head>
    <meta charset="utf-8">
    >title>Loop Academic</title>
    <link rel="stylesheet" href="https://stackpath.bootstrapcdn.com/bootstrap/4.3.1/css/bootstrap.min.css" integrity="sha384-ggOyR0iXCbMQv3Xipma34MD+dH/1fQ784/j6cY/iJTQUOhcWr7x9JvoRxT2MZw1T" crossorigin="anonymous">
    <link rel="stylesheet" href="https://stackpath.bootstrapcdn.com/bootstrap/3.4.1/css/bootstrap-theme.min.css" integrity="sha384-6pzBo3FDv/PJ8r2KRkGHifhEocL+1X2rVCTTkUfGk7/0pbek5mMa1upzvWbrUbOZ" crossorigin="anonymous">
    <link rel="stylesheet" href="system_style.css">
    <link rel="stylesheet" href="style.css">
    <link rel="stylesheet" href="https://cdnjs.cloudflare.com/ajax/libs/font-awesome/4.7.0/css/font-awesome.min.css">
    <meta name="viewport" content="width=device-width, initial-scale=1">
    <link rel="shortcut icon" href="Favicon.png" sizes="32x32" type="image/ico">
    
    <src="script_1.js"></script>
    <script src="https://code.jquery.com/jquery-3.3.1.slim.min.js" integrity="sha384-q8i/X+965DzO0rT7abK41JStQlAqVgRVzpbzo5smXKp4YfRvH+8abtTE1Pi6jizo" crossorigin="anonymous"></script>
    <script src="https://cdnjs.cloudflare.com/ajax/libs/popper.js/1.14.7/umd/popper.min.js" integrity="sha384-UO2eT0CpHqdSJQ6hJty5KVphtPhzWj9WO1clHTMGa3JDZwrnQq4sF86dIHNDz0W1" crossorigin="anonymous"></script>
    <script src="https://stackpath.bootstrapcdn.com/bootstrap/4.3.1/js/bootstrap.min.js" integrity="sha384-JjSmVgyd0p3pXB1rRibZUAYoIly6OrQ6VrjIEaFf/nJGzIxFDsf4x0xIM+B07jRM" crossorigin="anonymous"></script>
  </head>
  
  <body style="background-color: rgb(233, 233, 233)">
    <div class="container-fluid">
      <div class="row">
        <div class="col-1">
```

```html
            <id="back_set" href="material.html"><img src="Images/left-arrow.png">>p>back</p></a>
          </div>
          <div class="col-9">
            <div class="row justify-content-center">
              <section class="col-11" style="margin-top: 8%;">
                <div id="top_info">
                  <span>Page 1 of 5</span>
                  <h5>Video-Classroom: IF-ELSE Decision Structure</h5>
                </div>
                <div class="embed-responsive embed-responsive-21by9">
                  <iframe class="embed-responsive-item" src="https://www.youtube.com/embed/U8ixPxL54Sk" frameborder="0" allow="accelerometer; autoplay; encrypted-media; gyroscope; picture-in-picture" allowfullscreen></iframe>
                </div>
                <button class="back btn-light" type="button" disabled>< Anterior</button>
                <button class="next" onclick="window.location.href='material_2.html';" type="button">Próximo ></button>
              </section>
            </div>
          </div>


          <nav class="col-md-2 d-none d-md-block bg-dark sidebar">
            <div class="sidebar-sticky">
              >ul class="nav flex-column">
                <li class="nav-item">
                  <h5 style="color: white;">Content</h5><h4 style="color: white;">Programmatic</h4>
                </li>
                <li class="nav-item right_bar">
                  <div id="current_material">Current</div>
                  <class="nav-link active" style="background-color: white; color: black;" href="material_video.html">
                    <small>Video Classroom</small><p>IF-ELSE Decision Structure</p> <span class="sr-only">(current)</span>
                  </a>
                </li>
                <li class="nav-item right_bar">
                  <class="nav-link" href="material_2.html">
                    <small>VideoClassroom</small><p>Decision Structure SWITCH</p>
                  </a>
                </li>
                <li class="nav-item right_bar">
                  <class="nav-link" href="material_3.html">
                    <small>Mental Plate</small><p>Review - Decision Structures</p>
                  </a>
                </li>
                <li class="nav-item right_bar">
                  <class="nav-link" href="material_4.html">
                    <small>Archives</small><p>My Library</p>
                  </a>
                </li>
```

```html
            <li class="nav-item right_bar">
              <class="nav-link" href="material_5.html">
                <small>Video Classroom</small><p>Examples - Decision Structures</p>
              </a>
            </li>
        </ul>
      </div>
        </nav>
      </div>
  </body>
</html>
```

I want morebooks!

Buy your books fast and straightforward online - at one of world's fastest growing online book stores! Environmentally sound due to Print-on-Demand technologies.

Buy your books online at
www.morebooks.shop

Kaufen Sie Ihre Bücher schnell und unkompliziert online – auf einer der am schnellsten wachsenden Buchhandelsplattformen weltweit! Dank Print-On-Demand umwelt- und ressourcenschonend produziert.

Bücher schneller online kaufen
www.morebooks.shop

KS OmniScriptum Publishing
Brivibas gatve 197
LV-1039 Riga, Latvia
Telefax: +371 686 204 55

info@omniscriptum.com
www.omniscriptum.com

Lightning Source UK Ltd.
Milton Keynes UK
UKHW012020191121
394249UK00001B/74